The Renewing of
the Holy Ghost

The Renewing of the Holy Ghost

By Dr. Mark D. Hanby

Destiny Image® Publishers, Inc.
P.O. Box 351
Shippensburg, PA 17257-0351

"Speaking to the Purposes of God for This Generation and for the Generations to Come"

ISBN 1-56043-031-1

For Worldwide Distribution
Printed in the U.S.A.

Third Printing: 1996   Fourth Printing: 1998

This book and all other Destiny Image, Revival Press, and Treasure House books are available at Christian bookstores and distributors worldwide.

For a U.S. bookstore nearest you, call **1-800-722-6774**.
For more information on foreign distributors,
call **717-532-3040**.
Or reach us on the Internet: **http://www.reapernet.com**

Dedication

This book is dedicated to Reverend C. R. Free, who rescued my young pastorate by teaching me the principles of the renewing of the Holy Ghost.

Contents

Introduction

I can't remember when I lost interest in performance religion and actually ceased being concerned with everyone else's doctrinal issue, but I believe it was near the time I discovered how futile our conventional methods of evangelism were. This, along with my disdain for ministerial competition and a fervent urge to flee religious politics, left me with few professional crutches.

So, when I accepted my first pastorate at the tender age of twenty-three, I had already become an active member of the God seekers! My program for church growth and spiritual success consisted mainly of frequent fasts and prayer-filled days and nights.

The truth is that I had left myself so few options that the greatest proposition of my life simply became the pursuit of divine purpose.

While the great preachers spoke imposingly of the magnificent doors of revelation and explained with classic illustrations the weight of chains and locks, I was always scratching around on my hands and knees looking for keys.

One of the sages of our denomination encouraged me, however, by explaining to me that I really wasn't a rebel; and, in his own sweet way said, "You're a maverick ...there is a difference, you know!" I didn't know the difference and, for that matter, I really didn't know who or what I was.

I was convinced, however, that the church did not have to smell like a mortuary and sound like a five-hundred year old pipe organ.

My frustration was compounded by the constant prattle that our "group" had all the truth and that the whole world would have to come to us to find salvation.

I realized that, while we had been blessed to know many truths concerning the baptism, gifts and operations of the Holy Spirit, we had lost purpose and compassion, leaving us vulnerable to Phariseeism and hypocrisy.

The only way I found to release the straining geysers in my spirit was to preach "Revival, Revival, Revival – God wants to give a great last-day revival to the Church!"

I rose up out of the dust of spiritual confusion, holding a great key in my hand and heart. Revival would be the result of spiritual renewal! Thus was born the theme of this book: "The Renewing of the Holy Ghost."

Today, twenty years later, above the muttering of popular cliches and worn out illustrations, still comes the cry of a few divinely discontented souls searching to rediscover the boundless untapped resources of the full apostolic power. These are the spiritually hungry who have not yielded to the easy pace of average service accepted by the complacent majority.

If you are one of those, we've been looking for each other.

Mark D. Hanby

Chapter 1

The Renewing of the Holy Ghost

Not by works of righteousness which we have done, but according to his mercy he saved us, by the washing of regeneration and renewing of the Holy Ghost.

Titus 3:5

The lightning speed with which this tormented, tragically deceived generation is plunging toward eternity wrenches from the heart of every concerned Christian any desire for gospel 'games' or spiritual amusement. The burdened soul of the prayerful believer is left with only a lonely crying out to really know 'where went the power' of the early New Testament Church and the profundity of its gospel witness.

Somewhere, far away from our narrow religious prisons, surrounded by the dark, damp tunnels of denominational tradition, beckon the fresh, sweet paths of spiritual insight, leading to vast treasures of power and success.

Two of these lovely paths are outlined for us in our scriptural text, Titus 3:5.

> *Not by the works of righteousness which we have done, but according to his mercy he saved us, by the washing of regeneration and renewing of the Holy Ghost.*

Titus 3:5

First is REGENERATION. Next, THE RENEWING OF THE HOLY GHOST. Regeneration is what God does for us spiritually and supernaturally, while renewing is what we do for ourselves through seeking and pressing for deeper and closer experiences with our Lord.

One who claims only an initial experience in the Holy Spirit will soon become a stagnant pool, covered with the green slime of betterness and restless with the larvae of materialism, thus becoming a breeding place for discontent. In contrast, those who are consistently renewed are a refreshing fountain for thirsty souls.

In this chapter, let's examine regeneration[1] and its life-changing effect on the believer.

Regeneration is the accomplishment of Deity, stooping to salvage and rescue utterly doomed humanity. Oh what blessed relief! Old things are taken away and all things are made new! We have become new creatures in Christ Jesus. Without regeneration a man cannot be saved from pronounced judgment against all mankind.

Regeneration is the birth of water and the Spirit (John Chapter 3). It was preached on the day of Pentecost (Acts 2), introduced to the Gentiles (Acts 10), and ministered by Paul to the Ephesians (Acts 19).

We stand on the scriptural platform and declare that for a sinner to be saved from the error of his way, he must believe, as the "scripture hath said" (St. John 7:38), dying to sin

(Romans 6:6-9). He is then buried in a watery grave (Romans 6:1-4), and resurrected with Christ (Romans 6:5).

Believing the Gospel message and being saved (Acts 16:30-39) directly identifies the believer with the death, burial and resurrection of Jesus Christ (I Corinthians 15:1-4). Regeneration, then, is the death of the "old man" and the Genesis or beginning of a "new creature" in Christ! (II Corinthians 5:17-21)

Isn't it interesting that the determined love of the uninformed newcomer to this gospel truth has produced more for the cause of Christ and evangelism than the professional-type attitude of well-settled members? Somehow, we successfully manage to train out of our new converts the power and excitement that come to them with the glorious 'new birth' experience.

There is a basic instinct in an unspoiled, newborn saint that makes him love men, women, boys and girls, no matter what their station in life. When these newly baptized souls stagger up from a Salvation altar, they are often seen joyfully embracing those nearest them, crying, "Oh, I've got to go tell my family!" Now, give them a few months in our traditionally religious services, and we begin to see the waning of this great, innate desire, as we pull them farther and farther away into the tracks of routine effort that our wheels have traveled for so many years.

The enthusiasm and excitement of this first love in a newborn child of God once overlooked the discouraging facts and seeming impossibilities of soul-winning and said, "I must; I have to; they're lost!"

What is in the heart of a babe who seeks a mother's breast; or the instinct in the tiny songbird that opens its bill wide at the sound of a fluttering at the edge of the nest? Nature willingly bequeaths to these helpless, little creatures an inborn ability to pursue and obtain the life-source.

What is in a newborn believer who cries through the night for the lost relatives, prays throughout the day for unsaved companions, and sends an endless caravan of faith-packed, prayer requests to the pastor's desk for wayward sons and daughters? Are these the spastic motions or infantile responses of a spiritually unfocused mind? No! These spiritual babes are naturally obtaining and redistributing the life-source. They are born with the gospel principle: " ...freely ye have received, freely give." These fresh ones, whose eyes are not accustomed to our established procedures, look beyond the walls of our impossibilities and, with reckless faith, envision what we are 'confident' could never come to pass.

Many of these sucklings are thought to be suffering from a childhood disease. The symptoms are carefully observed by the healthy 'spiritual specialists': running eyes, dripping noses, unearthly groanings, frequent stammerings and repeated seizures. After a thorough examination, the diagnosis is blushingly reported in these words: "Well, he's new here. Please, don't be alarmed. The affliction at this stage is not contagious and, with 'proper religious treatment,' this zealous young'un will be completely cured in a few days."

I submit that this sweet, young child of God is not afflicted at all, but is still tender enough to let his heart be broken with the things that broke the heart of his Lord.

And when he (Jesus) saw the multitude he was moved with COMPASSION!
                                        Matthew 9:36

The new one is still able to put himself in the position of a sinner with empathy for his situation. Compassion is simply being able to say, "I know how you feel; you see, it's been just a few hours, a few days, or a few weeks since I was there. I remember the "pit from whence I was digged ... " (Isaiah 51:1). "I remember the sucking mire clinging to my ankles and knees, dragging me ever downward, toward a pit from which I could not extricate myself. I remember the lonely nights and the agonizing years of endless searching for hopes and joys that could not be found. I remember emptiness and waste, the lonely harbingers of death that knocked endlessly at my door, with no comforting advocate to put an arm around my shoulder."

The love and compassion in the heart of this newborn sensitively feel and remember every pang of sin and reach out to do what a long-time professional church member 'knows' cannot be done, because time and security have erased the painful memory of his wretched past. The comfortable "saint" has been drinking a long time at the fountain and often does not remember the desperate longing for one drop of cool water. He has long nibbled from tables laden with rich messages and the fresh fruit of constant encouragement. He's satisfied!

God prophetically sets Isaiah's warning alongside the foundation text foretelling the outpouring of the Holy Ghost.

> *Woe to the crown of pride, to the drunkards of É-phra-im, whose glorious beauty is a fading flower, which are on the head of the fat valleys of them that are overcome with wine!*
>
> Isaiah 28:1

Moses, the meek man of the Bible, endured the type and shadow for our example (I Corinthians 10:1-12), fervently warning these fat souls:

Hear, O Israel: The Lord our God is one Lord: And thou shalt love the Lord thine God with all thy heart, and with all thy soul, and with all thy might.

And these words, which I command thee this day, shall be in thine heart:

And thou shalt teach them diligently unto thy children, and shalt talk of them when thou sittest in thine house, and when thou walkest by the way, and when thou liest down, and when thou risest up.

And thou shalt bind them for a sign upon thine hand, and they shall be as frontlets between thine eyes.

And thou shalt write them upon the posts of thy house, and on thy gates.

And it shall be, when the Lord thy God shall have brought thee into the land which he sware unto thy fathers, to Abraham, to Isaac, and to Jacob, to give thee great and goodly cities, which thou buildedest not,

And houses full of all good things, which thou filledst not, and wells digged, which thou diggedst not, vineyards and olive

trees, which thou plantedst not; when
thou shalt have eaten and be full;
THEN BEWARE LEST THOU FORGET THE
LORD, WHICH BROUGHT THEE FORTH OUT
OF THE LAND OF EGYPT, FROM THE HOUSE
OF BONDAGE.

Deuteronomy 6:4-12

In sad consummation to a book full of messages and with a heart laden responsibility,
Moses finally penned these words:

Remember the days of old, consider the
years of many generations: ask thy
father, and he will shew thee; thy elders,
and they will tell thee.
When the most High divided to the na-
tions their inheritance, when he
separated the sons of Adam, he set the
bounds of the people according to the
number of the children of Israel.
For the Lord's portion is his people; Jacob
is the lot of his inheritance.
He found him in a desert land, and in the
waste howling wilderness; he led him
about, he instructed him, he kept him as

the apple of his eye.

As an eagle stirreth up her nest, fluttereth over her young, spreadeth abroad her wings, taketh them, beareth them on her wings:

So the Lord alone did lead him, and there was no strange god with him.

He made him ride on the high places of the earth, that he might eat the increase of the fields; and he made him to suck honey out of the rock, and oil out of the flinty rock;

Butter of kine, and milk of sheep, with fat of lambs, and rams of the breed of Bá-shan, and goats, with the fat of kidneys of wheat; and thou didst drink the pure blood of the grape.

BUT JE-SHU-RUN WAXED FAT AND KICKED: THOU ART WAXEN FAT, THOU ART GROWN THICK, THOU ART COVERED WITH FATNESS: THEN HE FORSOOK GOD WHICH MADE HIM, AND LIGHTLY ESTEEMED THE ROCK OF HIS SALVATION.

They provoked Him to jealousy with strange gods, with abominations provoked *they Him to anger.*

They sacrificed unto devils, not to God; to gods whom they know not, to new gods that came newly up, whom your fathers feared not. (Tradition)

OF THE ROCK THAT BEGAT THEE THOU ART UNMINDFUL, AND HAS FORGOTTEN GOD THAT FORMED THEE.

AND HE SAID, I WILL HIDE MY FACE FROM THEM, I WILL SEE WHAT THEIR END SHALL BE: FOR THEY ARE A VERY FORWARD GENERATION, CHILDREN IN WHOM IS NO FAITH.

Deuteronomy 32:7-18,20

Endnotes

1. Strongs - 3824 "(Verbatum)" from the root of 1078 "(Verbatum)" Genesis! beginning! Nativity!!

Chapter 2

The Absolute Necessity of Renewal

...And when they had prayed, the place was shaken where they were assembled together; and they were all filled with the Holy Ghost, and they spake the word of God with boldness.

Acts 4:31

Prayerless men, gossiping women, worldly young people, indifferent Sunday School teachers and disgruntled church boards, all totally barren of fruits and gifts of the Spirit, half-heartedly participate in joyless worship and browse daintily at our sterile altars. These should already have convinced us that the RENEWING OF THE HOLY GHOST is as important as that first baptism. How can we exist without the vital life-sign of spiritual reproduction, which according to God's Word, is the very reason for our existence? And how may we excuse the fact that our offensive against diseases and devils is pitifully weak and anemic? We are desperately in need of some substantial evidence as to the power and effect of our bold gospel.

Even with the healed crippled standing with them (Acts 4), obviously testifying of apostolic power and authority, Peter and John along with the other disciples, were driven to their knees by the insatiable thirst for renewal, thus giving us a living insight into their spiritual lifeline and secret for continued victory.

And when they had prayed, the place was shaken where they were assembled together; and they were all filled with the Holy Ghost, and they spake the word of God with boldness.

Acts 4:31

The once-born churches of Revelation received the pronouncement of judgment, not because of a bad start, but because of a mediocre follow-through. This eventual blight of lukewarmness could be cured only by a repeat of first works, after sincere repentance and a purchasing of heretofore unattained spiritual qualities in consecration.

Our modern Laodicean procedures may salve our bleeding consciences, but they do not brush aside the vindictive finger of judgment pointed by a glorified Savior at a self-justified church.

There is an **absolute necessity** of our constant reaching for a recharging and rebaptism of the initial experience. This renewing does not come automatically or by the process of time, but only as we show definite desire and exercise positive faith, as in our first all-out efforts to reach God.

Many of us have long *believed* that regeneration was necessary and mandatory but, somehow, have never been able to distinguish between renewing and regeneration. Both of these roads have been marked with a single sign, and we have been taught to believe that the renewing of the Holy Ghost is just 'praying through' again. This is, however, somewhat faulty in concept and definitely short of understanding. 'Praying through' may be 'keeping the Holy Ghost,' but the renewing of the Holy Ghost is a spiritual process of growth and maturity.

The fortunate parents of a healthy child are not altogether satisfied in the newborn remaining alive; they are anxiously concerned about his growth and development. These proud parents do not complain when their son outgrows his crib or when his last year's 'britches' come only to his knees. They gladly spend their wealth to change wardrobes, increase shoe sizes, pay lunch bills and buy note tablets for this healthy, growing youngster. These same loving guardians would be greatly distressed and most willing to seek any aid or remedy, upon learning that their child had reached an impasse in his journey toward complete, normal manhood and maturity.

So our heavenly Father is concerned with more than our birth. It is His desire and will that we:

...all come in the unity of the faith, and of the knowledge of the Son of God, unto a PERFECT MAN, unto the measure of the stature of the FULLNESS of Christ:

That we henceforth be no more CHILDREN, tossed to and fro, and carried about with every wind of doctrine, by the sleight of men, and cunning craftiness, whereby they lie in wait to deceive;

But speaking the truth in love, may GROW UP into him in all things, which is the head, even Christ;

From whom the whole body fitly joined together and compacted by that which every joint supplieth, according to the effectual working in the measure of every part, maketh INCREASE OF THE BODY unto the edifying of itself in love.

Ephesians 4:13-16

So then, the renewing of the Holy Ghost is as necessary as regeneration and, in understanding these spiritual principles and their individual functions and operations, lies the option of being a power-witness or being what we commonly consider 'a good saint.'

> For the invisible thing of him from the creation of the world are clearly seen, **being understood by the things that are made,** even his eternal power and Godhead; so that they are without excuse:
>
> Romans 1:20

Physiology (one of those things "being understood") has revealed to us many things about the human body. We are mainly interested, however, in the basic units of the body that give or take life.

Every basic part of the body is made up of a collection of tiny units called cells. These cells represent tiny chemical factories that constantly take in and transform certain raw materials and send out new and different substances. The raw materials and the finished products make their way out of the cell through the extremely thin membrane forming the cell wall.

It may be interesting to note that there are trillions of cells in your body; it is said that the red cells alone number some 25 trillion. Now just consider, beloved, that each one of our complex selves originated as a single cell–a fertilized egg. Scientists further inform us that all of our present cells were derived from that original cell by the process of cleavage, or division.

Lest we fall into the snare of the extreme wisdom by further discourse, suffice it to say that it is of great importance in the growth and development of the body, and in the maintenance and repair of the body (when it is full grown), that the process of cell division, replacement and renewal constantly take place. Cells are continually dying and being replaced in our bodies. Thousands of dead cells are washed from the surface of the skin every time we bathe, and it has been estimated that, during every second of our life, 100,000,000 red blood cells die and are replaced by new ones.

It is proven that every cell in the body is completely replaced and renewed every seven years. If the body does not receive the raw material with which to manufacture new cells, so that the process of renewing may continue, it cannot live more than a few days. The human body cannot live without renewal.

The process of renewing in lower animal life, commonly known as molting, is the replacement of skin or feathers by an animal. Some snakes and amphibians, for example, molt about once a month. The feared and respected rattlesnake leaves his skin among the rocks of his lair. Nearly all birds shed and replace their feathers during the annual molt which usually takes place in late summer. 'Lost' feathers don the caps of scouting youngsters. Some birds also have a second molt in the spring before the beginning of their productive season. With each molt the coloring of the plumage may change and the bird may go into partial retirement. You will remember the farmer's common friend, the hen, whose feathers drop out a few at a time, and in definite order, so that the bird appears ragged and shedding.

The value of the cycle of seasons, sowing and reaping, is taught by agriculture (another of those things "being understood"). It is impossible for the farmer to reap a crop until he has first cut down the stalks of last year's corn, plowed them back into the soil, and smoothed the dirt for another year's planting. The chaff is scattered before the wheat can be planted again, and the apples in the orchard must fall to the ground before new fruit can come.

Modern Technology, understanding the "things that are made," also teaches us the necessity of renewal. No automobile manufacturer, with all his ingenuity, has yet designed a vehicle with a fuel capacity to last the lifetime of a car. One of the most affluent enterprises in the world is the common filling station industry; extensive travel is impossible without it.

Consider a modern aircraft that may carry 300-plus passengers half-way around the world. The burst of power at take-off and the whisper-smooth ride thousands of feet above our terra firma would be only a frustrating and pointless experience if, at its destination, there were no facilities for replenishing the power supply. With no refueling, the plane would become useless, a favorite target of the elements, a nesting place for sparrows. Great speeches extolling the virtues, power, and possibilities of this multimillion-dollar manifestation of technological achievement would be lost and tarnished like the oxidizing of its silver sides, if the power had been dissipated and there were no sources of renewal.

Replaced cells, ugly hides, and ragged feathers are all part of nature's mute testimony that renewing is absolutely necessary; without it, none can live. Renewal is the on-going process of life.

Renewing takes from us the 'snakeskin' of deceit, the 'feathers' of hypocrisy and the 'plumage' of pride. As the trees of the orchard are of no value, unless their fruit is shared with others, so the rotten 'pulp' of self-centeredness must be stripped from our branches. Consider the surrendering stalks in the field; so our past accomplishments, successes, and personal achievements must willingly be plowed under to give richness to a new, spring crop.

With hearts pulverized by this mighty preaching and our souls disheleved by conviction, we tearfully succumb to the words of the prophet:

Therefore also now, saith the Lord, turn ye even to me with ALL your heart, and with fasting, and with weeping, and with mourning;

And REND YOUR HEART, and not your garments, and turn unto the Lord your God; for he is gracious and merciful, slow to anger, and of great kindness, and repenteth him of the evil.

Who knoweth if he will return and repent, and leave a blessing behind him; even a meat offering and a drink offering unto the Lord your God?

Blow the trumpet in Zion, sanctify a fast, call a solemn assembly;

Gather the people, sanctify the congregation, assemble the elders, gather the children, and those that suck the breasts; let the bridegroom go forth of his chamber, and the bride out of her closet.

Let the priests, the ministers of the Lord, weep between the porch and the altar, and let them say, Spare thy people, O Lord, and give not thine heritage to reproach, that the heathen should rule over them; wherefore should they say among the people, Where is their God?

Joel 2:12-17

But these ragged mourners are not without the promise of renewing's benefits!

Be glad then, ye children of Zion, and rejoice in the Lord your God: for he hath given you the former rain moderately, and he will cause to come down for you the rain, the former rain, and the latter rain in the first month.

And the floors shall be full of wheat, and the fats shall overflow with wine and oil.

And I will restore to you the years that the locust hath eaten, the cankerworm, and the caterpillar, and the palmerworm, my great army which I sent among you.

And ye shall eat in plenty, and be satisfied, and praise the name of the

Lord your God, that hath dealt wondrously with you: and my people shall never be ashamed.

And ye shall know that I am in the midst of Israel, and that I am the Lord your God, and none else: and my people shall never be ashamed.

And it shall come to pass AFTER-WARD, that I will pour out my spirit upon all flesh ...!

Joel 2:23-28

Chapter 3

From Glory to Glory

But we all, with open face beholding as in a glass the glory of the Lord, are changed into the same image from glory to glory, even as by the Spirit of the Lord.

II Corinthians 3:18

Perhaps each of us could be likened to one who has just tumbled off the precipice of time into the swollen, raging tide of this generation, being carried swiftly toward its eternity. A drowning man will clutch at any object on the surface, when trying to keep his head above the water.

The initial experience in the Holy Spirit was a welcome limb, supporting our weight and rescuing us from certain death. However, we have been in this stream for some time. Our boots are full of water, our clothes are soaked, and the limb isn't nearly as valuable in supporting weight as it was at that first plunge. We need something more–something bigger–something with more security.

It is perplexing for us to leave something that has been precious and valuable, in order that we may find something else; but the Scripture teaches us that we go " ...from glory to glory" (II Corinthians 3:18). We must be willing to leave something good to gain something better. The principle of renewal, working in us, demands that we let go of complete dependence in past experiences. With trembling hands, we release the death grip of our initial baptism that we may flounder, plunge, and swim toward the log of greater glory, drifting a few arm lengths from our present situation.

We must come to a crisis. We must be willing to give away what we have, that we might gain something more; this is the principle of Heaven.

For God so love the world that he gave ...
                                    John 3:16

Is Heaven poorer for His giving? We rejoice with John as the messenger comes to him, arms laden with wrath and destruction, and leads him into the city to be introduced to the Bride, the Lamb's wife; (Revelation 21:9) Heaven is richer for His giving, and so are we! The whole principle is established: WE GET BY GIVING!

He that findeth his life shall lose it: and he that loseth his life for my sake shall find it.

Matthew 10:39

We go from victory to victory. We must leave Samaria's revival to save the eunuch in the desert (Acts 8). We must let go of the limb to gain the log. Then we balance, tottering and teetering precariously on the log, paying the price, and taking the chance to reach the over-hanging branches that will save us from the pounding falls.

Many timid souls are not willing to leave the victories of the past, and continue to testify and talk of those blessed things that happened to them years ago. But those renewed in the Holy Ghost will talk of the present power and glory of God, proclaiming the wonderful things happening NOW and the victories that are coming in the near future. They have been willing to go from victory to victory and from glory to glory.

We are the spiritual elect to God and prophetically will be gathered from the four distinct and different winds, which the Bible declares will blow at some time upon each of us.

And then shall he send his angels, and shall gather together his elect from the four winds, from the uttermost part of the earth to the uttermost part of heaven.

Mark 13:27

The East wind of chastening (Hosea 13:15), the West wind of blessings (Exodus 10:17-19), the North wind of cleansing (Job 37:21-24), and the South wind of renewal (Job 37:14-17), must sometime come to every one of God's elect.

Solomon, in his Song of Love (Song of Solomon 4:16), shows us the espoused bride standing in her withered garden, when she senses the nearness of her coming groom. She does not cry for chastening, (East wind) nor for blessings (West wind); but the urgent voice of the end-time bride wails out:

AWAKE, O north wind; and come, thou south; blow upon my garden, that the spices thereof may flow out ...

The North wind was Job's wind that passed and cleansed him, bringing God to him with all of His terrible majesty–the God that Job 'could not find out.' It brought His excellent power, judgment, and justice, and a definite fear and respect (Job 37). The North wind was Ezekiel's wind that brought deity to him in the striking, fiery amber and power that smote Ezekiel to the ground (Ezekiel 1:4,27,28).

The espoused bride knew that raisins could not pass for lush grapes and that dried prunes upon the vine would not be acceptable as sweet plums. She knew that the shriveled fruit beneath the brown branch and the dying leaf would not be pleasant for her beloved to eat. She had to be willing for the cold, chilling

North wind, that drives the ducks from the ponds, the leaves from the trees, and the brown grass into the soil, to come and strip her garden, until it stood empty and alone, with nothing but the promise of the South wind.

The South wind is the wind for going (Acts 27:13), the wind of refreshing and renewing. It is the wind that awoke in the heart of seamen the desire to put their ships to sea, discover new ports, and to explore pleasant islands. The South wind woos the spring rains that fall softly upon the cultivated tracts, causing the small seeds in the soil to burst forth, sending green shoots upward toward the sun. Only after a long, hard, cold winter can a farmer appreciate the small blade of grass or a tiny leaf of corn. After the winter's chill, he is so excited that he may drop to his knees, examining the first showing of green across the wintered field.

The North wind has driven everything but memory away, and now comes the renewing. The new world is sweet and fresh, all things come to life again. The feelings that once died in the farmer, through familiarity, are now vibrantly renewed. Where once he strolled carelessly through the fields, tramping down the familiar stalks, not careful for the moaning of the common plants, he now places his feet very carefully between the tender rows. The heart of the husbandman "thrills with the song of spring" (James 5:7). He has been willing to leave one victory to come to another. After suffering the North winds, the renewing again brings to him that *"first love,"* THE ONLY HOPE OF THE CHURCH!

The cry of the espoused bride, in hearing the footfall of her coming lover, is not for blessings, nor for wealth, but that she may be stripped of all past benefits and be renewed with lush new fruit, that her lover may find her garden pleasant to eat from.

The renewing of the Holy Ghost is God's "Shibboleth" to the church (Judges 12). It is the watchword of life or death! Renewing brings a sense of emergency to the church. Strickened members moan with their heads under the altar, as though they had never known God at all. Young people in the congregation lay on their faces, groaning out spiritual utterances–in repentance expressing their pain and grief. Pastors find themselves staring blindly at the people with a haunting emptiness in their souls, strangling at times on the very words they try to moralize. Eventually, the once well-satisfied, comfortable congregation becomes a ragged nest of mourning, searching, dying people, striking out wildly from the limb of salvation to the log of renewing. Floundering, flailing, coughing and choking, where once they were at ease and secure, they now chance life, to find its deeper meaning.

The bland messages that have been warbled over and over again unexpectedly become choking sobs, as the ministers weep between the porch and the altar, standing pleadingly between God and men. Tact is flung to the winds, and arguments for security disappear. Past blessings and accomplishments are completely obliterated by rivers of salty tears. The unconcerned and the hypocrites become sadly more outstanding by their refusal to participate, and every church service seems to be paced by the chiming of the bells of eternity.

The phrase "inherit the wind" (Proverbs 11:29), reveals the principle that rewards, especially evil rewards, will come in time. Many modern day Christians, however, passively insist that greater glory and victory may be "inherited" by those who wait. These drowsy souls have immortalized the phrase 'when God gets ready,' and have evasively omitted "the violent take the kingdom by force" (Matthew 11:12).

Beware! We haven't time for pleasant zephyrs to awake and aid us at their leisure. The coming of our groom is at hand! We observe His approach through the sooty mirrors and darkened glasses of this hell-bound generation. In gutteral tones of anguish we should plead:

Oh, blessed wind of Pentecost, where did you make your bed in this dark night of sin. Holy wind of Apostolic boldness, our churches are unshaken in your absence. WAKE UP, OH WINDS, and gust into our sanctuaries, levelling our idols of tradition and ripping down our proud banners of apathy.

Now, "the God seekers" fill hours with tear-ful prayers; men leave their jobs and come home early because of crushing burdens. Ladies abandon their washings to kneel beside the couch, battling to gain a new place in God. Young people tearfully look for closets of prayer.

It's happening! Fresh testimonies are burst-ing forth. Reports of spiritual healing sweep in! The entire church is abruptly caught up in a vast feeling of revival. No one is talking about the "good old days," for everybody is con-sciously aware of the present power and *renewing of the Holy Ghost!*

The sound of the dresser's axe rings clearly throughout his vineyard! His pitiful voice speaks.

Behold these three years I come seeking fruit on this fig tree and find none ...

With a sign of resignation he regretfully an-nounces:

...cut it down!

Luke 13:6-9

Alas! Necessity is laid upon us; we must be rebaptized. As Rachel mourned for children and would not be comforted:

...*Give me children or else I die.*
Genesis 30:1

So may we sorrow for our fruitlessness.

RENEW ME OR I DIE !

Chapter Four

Wells and Cisterns

Be astonished, O ye heavens, at this, and be horribly afraid, be ye very desolate, saith the Lord.
For my people have committed two evils; they have forsaken me the fountain of living waters, and hewed them out cisterns, broken cisterns, that can hold no water.

Jeremiah 2:12-13

Having much mercy upon the author's poor ability at mental artistry, let us all patiently 'gather round' in an attempt to decipher the meaning of the following illustration.

The next time you stand in your congregation, try to imagine the auditorium as an open

field and each individual member as repre-
senting a hollow, sunken cylinder, like a hand-
dug well.

Please disregard the fact that they all look
similar externally and consider that all of them
fall into one of two distinctively opposite
categories. Each regular member, is either a
WELL or a CISTERN.

There is an all-important difference between a well and a cistern.

A WELL has a source within itself and flows
ever upward and outward, bathing its sur-
roundings in cool, refreshing, life-giving water.
Jesus spoke of these wells saying:

> ...but the water that I shall give him
> shall be in him a well of water springing
> up into everlasting life.
>
> St. John 4:14

In sharp contrast, the CISTERN has all the
possibilities of being a well–except that the in-
ward supply is gone. These empty souls have
forsaken the "fountain of living water." Their
walls are soon cracked by dryness, neglect,

and self-hewn philosophies so that even when filled by some external supply, as they must be if they possess anything at all, the water is lost into the black humus of their carnal hearts. Indifferently, these spongers wait in motionless satisfaction for some spiritual well to overflow and again moisten the thirsty abyss of their souls.

Jude beheld these and with unbridled candor, penned this searing rebuke:

These are spots in your feasts of charity, when they feast with you, feeding themselves without fear: clouds they are without water, carried about of winds; trees whose fruits withereth, without fruit, twice dead, plucked up by the roots;
Raging waves of the sea, foaming out their own shame; wandering stars, to whom is reserved the blackness of darkness for ever.
These be they who separate themselves ("They have forsaken me, the fountain of living waters, and have hewed them out cisterns, broken cisterns, that can hold no water"), *sensual, HAVING NOT THE SPIRIT.*
Jude 12-13,19

Nor could the insidious spiritual crime of the cisterns be overlooked by the apostle with the keys; for Peter said:

*These are **wells without water,** clouds that are carried with a tempest: to whom the mist of darkness is reserved for ever.*
                                   II Peter 2:17

For it had been better for them not to have known the way of righteousness, than, after they have known it, to turn from the holy commandment delivered unto them.
                                   II Peter 2:21

There is a river, the streams whereof shall make glad the city of God, the holy place of the tabernacles of the most High.
                                   Psalms 46:4

He that believeth on me, as the scripture hath said, out of his belly shall flow rivers of living water.
                                   St. John 7:38

What? know ye not that your body is the temple of the Holy Ghost which is in you,

*which ye have of God, and ye are not your
own?*

I Corinthians 6:19

Very little research is needed to arrive at the conclusion that a well is not dug for the mere pleasure of digging, and that it was never meant to be a satisfaction to itself alone. No matter how elaborately the well-cap may be fashioned or how elegantly the springhouse may be designed, the most worthy reason for a well's existence is that it shares its water.

These scriptures teach us that, out of the tabernacles (temples, wells, and innermost beings), shall come a river driven by the force of many tributaries. Each source is a singular well, pouring its precious substance into a torrent of unity, coursing its way through the desert to the sea.

Ezekiel was led in vision one day past the door of the House of the Lord (typical, perhaps, of our present church facilities):

...and, behold, waters issued out from under the threshold of the house eastward: for the forefront of the house

stood toward the east, and the waters came down from under from the right side of the house, at the south side of the altar.

Then brought he me out of the way of the gate northward, and led me about the way without unto the utter gate by the way that looketh eastward; and, behold, there ran out waters on the right side.

And when the man that had the line in his hand went forth eastward, he measured a thousand cubits, and he brought me through the waters; the waters were to the ankles.

Again he measured a thousand, and brought me through the waters; the waters were to the knees. Again he measured a thousand, and brought me through; the waters were to the loins.

Afterward he measured a thousand; and it was a river that I could not pass over; for the waters were risen, waters to swim in, a river that could not be passed over.

And He said unto me, Son of man, hast thou seen this? Then he brought me, and caused me to return to the brink of the river.

Now when I had returned, behold, at the bank of the river were very many trees on the one side and on the other.

Then said he unto me, these waters issue out toward the east country, and go down into the desert, and go into the sea: which being brought forth into the sea, the waters shall be healed.

And it shall come to pass, that everything that liveth, which moveth, withersoever the rivers shall come, shall live: and there shall be a very great multitude of fish, because these waters shall come thither; for they shall be healed; and everything shall live wither the river cometh.

Ezekiel 47:1-9

After being spiritually enlightened by the prophet's challenging vision, who among us would not humbly confess that there are multitudes of fish (people) in our sea (city) who will never be reached by our present mechanical witness or powerless presentations. They are longing, languishing and dying, waiting for the flowing of a river. Lonely executives, weary housewives, sensation-addicted youths and disgusted church members, though hiding behind a pretense of self-sufficiency, still unconsciously beg for living water. Isn't it a shame, that we can't get this life-giving substance past our cisterns?

Perhaps now we can see why Jeremiah spoke fervently and with fear. The Lord did not anoint him to say, "the religious people have made a mistake," but rather, "MY PEOPLE have SINNED." To be a cistern is not merely a fault; it is evil (Jeremiah 2:13).

Well, the ladies are chattering and the men are swapping stories, while their young'uns skip impishly through the aisles scattering songbooks, or plucking choice morsels of used bubble gum from the underside of well-carved pews. Giddy young people zealously prepare many precious strips of paper on which to smuggle their romantic notes across the congregation. Sorrowfully, somewhere in the background, from a tiny Sunday School room, the faithful few send up a series of odd moans in an attempt to gain a belated spiritual victory. It's Sunday morning and the Wells and Cisterns are gathering!

I wonder … have we forgotten the thirsty masses beyond the empty wastes of pleasure and sin, eagerly awaiting the sound of rushing water (Job 6:14-20)?

By contrast, as Ezekiel passed the door of the House of the Lord (his church), a trickle of water issued out from under the threshold. When he crossed the first time, the water was ankle-deep. Upon returning, after a time, the prophet found that the flow had risen to his knees; and again when he came by, the water was to his loins. In the final crossing, the waters were risen until there were " …WATERS TO SWIM IN, a river that could not be passed over" (Ezekiel 47:5).

It has never been the plan of God for His people to assemble only to get their 'bucket full.' The church has, since its birth, been intended to execute a particular PURPOSE in this world; the New Testament states it like this:

These signs shall follow them that believe.
                                        Mark 16:17

And they went forth, and preached every-where, the Lord working with them, and confirming the word with signs following.
                                        Mark 16:20

Pouring over the threshold of the upper room, into the streets, the members of the first church filled Jerusalem with the river of their doctrine and turned their world upside down! It is, inescapably, our responsibility to produce enough water within the sanctuary to cause a flood to burst out of the door, cascading into the streets, so that the Spirit of God may flow into every highway, thoroughfare, alley and byway, preparing the way and convicting souls of their overwhelming need for salvation.

Well, since it's church time, we will again dutifully set out to produce some living water. Yet, even while we prime a few faithful wells, our enthusiasm is short-lived; for, to our help-less dismay, as we view the field, we observe that all the painfully-gained substance we are managing to produce trickles only a few feet before splattering into the cavity of a gaping cistern that personally produces nothing.

Meanwhile, the steps of our church remain unmoistened by any spiritual overflow, and every powerful act of the Spirit is completely absorbed by those who prefer spiritual feasting to spiritual conquest. This tragic picture demands an honest answer to an honest question: of what lasting value are a few wells to a lost world, if their most extreme effort in production is completely and selfishly devoured within their own sanctuary walls?

We often encourage ourselves by saying, "We had a wonderful meeting tonight"; and it may be true, at the climax of the service, after pumping, priming and preaching, we are able to say that all were blessed by the Spirit, and everybody went home rejoicing. But what about the next service night, when we all congregate for good ole' Bible study? The cisterns will have successfully soaked away their blessings, and our tiresomely repetitious task begins once more. While the world waits longingly for the sound of water, we can't get it past the door.

We MUST overcome the balance of power. We MUST have more wells than cisterns. Do not despair, however, this can quickly be accomplished by the Holy Ghost renewal of the long inactive spiritual fountainhead within the cisterns of your congregation.

After this welcome increase in pumping power, those non-producing remaining few, as there seemingly always will be, can quickly be replenished by the rapidly rising surge. Waters then gush from our doors, terracing down the steps, plunging into the homes of hard-hearted and spiritually starving church attenders. We have vaulted into the realm of the Supernatural. The Spirit of the Lord is going where we could not go before and doing what we could not do!

Our activity in the Spirit is no longer an endless task of filling cisterns; the water is now flowing from one cylinder to another, but this time to be met by a similarly powerful force. These streams all join together, building a unified strength until suddenly:

> *...there is a river, the streams whereof shall make glad the city ...*
>
> **Psalms 46:4**

In the past, we have battled frantically, struggling against unbelievable odds, to spread this gospel. Our extreme effort to convince unbelievers and professional rejectors has met with constant and bewildering failure, until we have become satisfied with only the faintest motion forward.

But something new is happening now. Out of the individual tabernacles of the Holy Ghost issue bubbling springs, merging to form a sweeping river. Those we could not convince before, though evading us personally, are unexpectedly finding themselves sloshing through water they did not ask for. Whereas they could easily withstand the onslaught of our verbal bombasts, having managed to dispel each convicting message, they cannot cope with water that seeps under their doors, flooding bedrooms and kitchens. They find no rest at night and are strangely absent from their places at dinnertime. The river has enveloped them.

Meanwhile, among the regular members, chronic illnesses and afflictions are miraculously disappearing, and a greater percentage of folks prayed for are healed. Testimony services yield up these exciting reports:

Yesterday, my mother and father listened for the first time to my testimony. My husband is coming Sunday, to find God.

The pastor's message is only minutes old when a young man rudely interrupts by screaming, "I must be saved tonight!" The molested service comes to a screeching halt, as men repent, women weep, and saints team into prayer groups all about the auditorium. The enduring virus of infectious faith contagiously races through the congregation, dispelling doubt and encouraging unpremeditated spiritual recklessness. Chronic seekers easily receive the baptism of the Holy Ghost, causing spiritual riots at our congested altars.

Revival has come: we have overcome the balance of power! The water has "over-flowed the hiding place" (Isaiah 28:17), and the church has found its apostolic unction. When those once immobile church members are sarcastically questioned, "Can any good thing come out of Nazareth (THAT church)? They enthusiastically retort, "Come and see!" (John 1:46)

Now we are not putting our blistered hands to the plow alone. We are "laborers together with God" (I Corinthians 3:4).

...the Spirit AND the bride say, Come. And let him that heareth say, Come. And let him that is athirst come. And whosoever will, let him take the water of life freely.
Revelation 22:17

Each consecutive service is not a repeat of the previous cycle of priming, but continues with gushing power where we left off. Our once dry sanctuary has become a pool of clear water, and every street in our city is a stream.

Chapter Five

Love Finds a Way

Though I speak with the tongues of men and of angels, and have not charity, I am become as sounding brass, or a tinkling cymbal.

I Corinthians 13:1

A great percentage of all soul-winning done in the average evangelical church is accomplished, not by veteran members, but rather by new converts who have been saved six months or less!

Properly speaking, this situation defies all normal logic and bespeaks serious spiritual imbalance. In our quest for understanding, however, the causes behind this astonishing paradox are more clearly understood when we remember the sweet relief of righteousness, overwhelming peace and tremendous joy that accompanied our own initial baptism, firing us with a frantic urgency.

OH, BLESSED FIRST LOVE! What beckoning call of evening wooed you to take your flight from my lean and hungry soul?

The untrained spiritual children teach us that soul-winning is not an educated art or concept, nor can it be guaranteed by following a set of rules. It must be the result of something personal and powerful stirring within us. The weak, retreating disciples in Gethsemane became the powerful, mountain-moving patriarchs of the newborn Church after receiving the Holy Ghost. These formerly bewildered disciples, recognizing their own inability to fulfill the kingly charge of their departing master, "Go ye into ALL the world and preach the gospel to EVERY CREATURE" (Mark 16:15), tenaciously clung to this solitary ray of hope: "Ye shall receive POWER after that the Holy Ghost is come upon you …and ye SHALL BE witnesses unto me …" (Acts 1:8)

The common church member today usually comes to soul-winning class well-armed, and doesn't hesitate long before exploding with a number of excuses with which he is obsessed. Hiding his slothfulness, carelessness and faithlessness, he offers these remarks as an answer for his fruitlessness:

"I have a shy nature."

"I never have been able to talk to people."

"You know I'm very reserved."

"I don't think we should push people."

"The folks on my block are just not interested."

"I live in a strange neighborhood."

"My job's had me tied down lately."

"I just can't get my housework finished, and I think it's more important to keep a home than to be out beating the streets all day."

"My children demand so much of my time."

"It seems to me that all we do is go to church; aren't we ever supposed to have any time for ourselves and our family?"

"I've tried and tried, and it's no use."

"The Lord didn't call me to knock on

doors."

"I thought we paid the preacher to do the visiting."

"I couldn't sell a glass of water to a man dying of thirst. Let Henry do it. He could sell a snowball to an Eskimo!"

It seems they have forgotten the old scriptural adage, " ... If any man will come after me, let him deny himself, and take up his cross daily, and follow me" (Luke 9:23).

> *He that loveth father or mother more than me is not worthy of me: and he that loveth son or daughter more than me is not worthy of me. And he that taketh not his cross, and followeth after me is not worthy of me.*
>
>   Matthew 10:37-38

Many try to make their excuses sound legitimate by using justifiable, normal human activity as a 'reason' for not attending to God's spiritual business. The Lord, however, is certainly neither fooled nor impressed by those who constantly fabricate excuses, and He exposes both the fallacy of and judgment for their un-righteous activity in Luke 14:16-24.

> *Then said he unto him, A certain man made a great supper, and bade many:*
> *And sent his servant at supper time to say to them that were bidden, Come; for all things are now ready.*
> *And they all with one consent BEGAN TO MAKE EXCUSE. The first said unto him, I have bought a piece of ground, and I must needs go and see it: I pray thee have me excused.*
> *And another said, I have bought five yoke of oxen, and I go to prove them: I pray thee have me excused.*
> *And another said, I have married a wife, and therefore I cannot come.*
> *So that servant came, and shewed his lord these things. Then the master of the house being angry said to his servant, Go out quickly into the streets and lanes of the city, and bring in hither the poor, and the maimed, and the halt, and the blind.*
> *And the servant said, Lord, it is done as thou hast commanded, and yet there is room.*
> *And the lord said unto the servant, Go out*

*into the highways and hedges, and compel
them to come in, that my house may be
filled.*
*For I say unto you, That none of those men
which were bidden shall taste of my supper.*

We are compassionately and clearly
warned by this parable that the Lord cannot
accept this type of excuse but will, rather,
choose a different group of people to replace
those who were first bidden to the supper.

Few will argue against the right of a man to
buy and inspect a piece of land, and it is un-
reasonable to ask that a farmer not try the
oxen he has purchased. And who among us
would deny a man the blessing of spending
time with his wife and family? However, these
fine activities become mere baseless excuses
when offered as reasons for not obeying the
commandments of our Lord, such as:

*Thou shalt love the Lord thy God with ALL
thy heart, and with ALL thy soul, and
with ALL thy mind. This is the first and
great commandment.*
                          Matthew 22:37-38

Such a fervent and comprehensive state-
ment brings again to our minds one of the
'Laws of Grace':

> *But seek ye first the kingdom of God, and
> his righteousness: and all these things
> shall be added unto you.*
>
> Matthew 6:33

All decent and upright things may be done,
in proper time and in proper order. But NOTH-
ING takes pre-eminence over our responsibility
to save lost and dying men.

No man tells the river where to flow or the
wind where to blow. The river does not wait
for hills to be moved or for valleys to be dug.
It automatically flows to the lowest point, and
the rushing of its power sends its streams
around hindrances, over insurmountable
obstacles, and through thickets that even a
rabbit could not negotiate. Tumbling before it
that tattered debris, the watercourse carves
out a channel on its way to the oceans.
Though crooked and twisting, we may be sure
that the river always finds a way!

The third chapter of Acts discloses to us the story of the healing of a lame man at the Beautiful Gate, followed by the unparalleled preaching of Peter, when he brazenly condemned the sons of Abraham for denying the Holy and Just One and accepting a murderer, instead. He further denounced them for killing the Prince of Life and then excited them with the unbelievable tale that God actually raised Him from the dead. The bold fisherman refused to apologize for being a witness of that resurrection and further commanded every hearer to repent and be converted.

Peter then explained to all of the inquirers and agnostics that through the name of Jesus the lame man had been made well. Blazing into the fourth chapter, the uneducated Simon Peter, filled with the Holy Ghost and fire, delivered an invincible rebuttle against the stuffy high priests and scribes, by majestically unveiling the foundation truth that the unorthodox stone which was set at naught by the religious world of his day had become the Head of the corner.

With this torrent of condemnation blasting their bitter hearts, the chief priests took counsel as to how they might rid themselves of these fearless preachers. Now, it seems that the overwhelming influence of the religious leaders of that day should have easily out-maneuvered and stopped the mouths of these simple fishermen. When these stung high officials threatened and commanded them not to speak or teach at all in the name of Jesus, that warning should have been enough.

With a lion-like boldness these illbred, uncouth laborers fearlessly faced the elite mob who had successfully executed their Master and, with the Spirit surging like a pounding surf in their hearts, the disciples explained their usual position saying in effect, "We can't help it. We cannot but speak the things which we have seen and heard." SILENCE IS IMPOSSIBLE!

Hence we are instructed, by example, that soul-winning is not a rule that can be made or dictated but, rather, a result of uncapped spiritual pressure built up in the hearts of conscientious and concerned men and women. At any given time, in any given place, this inner fire may erupt into a POWERFUL WITNESS of what Jesus Christ has done, and is now doing.

Love for mankind in the heart of a true believer is not a passive feeling but an active energy.

It is no more possible for a renewed man or woman to be silent about the power of salvation than for a skinny branch to support the weight of a flying elephant, or a single man, by himself, to throw a dam across the mighty Amazon. Can one person stop an avalanche by spreading out his arms, or has history shown us a man who has harnessed the winds and tied them at his feet? Could we, by thinking, drain the oceans dry or move the mighty Teton Mountains to the east? Can a child pick up a fallen oak and stand it in its place again, or can a mother bring to life her stillborn babe? Nay! So neither can circumstances, ridicule, excuses or any other reason stop the POWER WITNESS of a spiritually renewed child of God!

Let us take a moment, now, and slow our restless attention to a thinker's walk; to be spiritually wise we must "let these things sink down into our ears" (Luke 9:43-45), hearing what the "SPIRIT sayeth to the churches." There is no debate about God's knowing our uncertain works, the pertinent question is, however: do we understand the simple meaning of the Spirit, as when Jesus pointedly declared that the very gates of Hell could not withstand the righteous bombardment of a glorious Church?

Have we then hidden our timid spirits among the shallow rushes of passive acceptance, whimpering that revival days are past? Are we sighing, "Just so we can somehow manage to hang on till He comes?"

We must rise up for these slimy pallets; our patient Master "hath somewhat against us!" He did not ask degrees of education or worlds of understanding, only a fresh new FIRST LOVE. We also clearly understand that any means or methods proposed without love are not only impractical, but utterly useless.

Though I speak with the tongues of men and of angels, and have not charity, I am

become as sounding brass, or a tinkling cymbal.
And though I have the gift of prophecy, and understand all mysteries, all knowledge; and though I have all faith, so that I could remove mountains, and not charity, I am nothing.
And though I bestow all my goods to feed the poor, and though I give my body to be burned, and have not charity, it profiteth me nothing."

I Corinthians 13:1-3

Promising crowns, thrones and worlds without end to all who will follow Him, our magnificent Lord omnipotently strides to the forefront of this generation's seething holocaust and sternly reminds our cowering hearts of the unlimited apostolic power lying dormant with us.

Behold, I give unto you power to tread on serpents and scorpions, and over all the power of the enemy: and nothing shall by any means hurt you.

Luke 10:19

Heal the sick, cleanse the lepers, raise the dead, cast out devils: freely ye have received, freely give.

Matthew 10:8

With love twisting their manly hearts, Peter and John found time for a begging cripple (on their way to prayer meeting) and delivered to him a portion of the power they personally possessed: "Such as I have give I thee." Nothing more was needed, and nothing less would suffice.

Love does not seek for assistance, only for acceptance. Without it, we shall always find excuses; and with it, we will always find a way.

Other *exciting titles* by Dr. Mark Hanby

YOU HAVE NOT MANY FATHERS
by Dr. Mark Hanby with Craig Ervin.
Explore with Dr. Hanby the relationship of father and son as the foundational connection for all spiritual impartation. As we turn our hearts toward one another, we will recover our heritage of generational blessing and double-portion anointing!
Paperback Book, 256p. ISBN 1-56043-166-0 Retail $9.99

THE HOUSE THAT GOD BUILT
Beyond whatever man can desire is a God-given pattern for the life of the Church. Here Dr. Hanby unfolds practical applications from the design of the Tabernacle that allow us to become the house God is building today.
Paperback Book, 140p. ISBN 1-56043-091-5 Retail $9.99

PERCEIVING THE WHEEL OF GOD
On the potter's wheel, a lump of clay yields to a necessary process of careful pressure and constant twisting. Similarly, the form of true faith is shaped by a trusting response to the hand of God in a suffering situation. This book offers essential understanding for victory through the struggles of life.
Paperback Book, 112p. ISBN 1-56043-109-1 Retail $9.99

ANOINTING THE UNSANCTIFIED
The anointing is more than a talented performance or an emotional response. In this book, Dr. Hanby details the essential ingredients of directional relationship that allow the Spirit of God to flow down upon the Body of Christ—and from us to the needs of a dying world.
Paperback Book, 196p. ISBN 1-56043-071-0 Retail $9.99

Available at your local Christian bookstore.
Internet: http://www.reapernet.com
Prices subject to change without notice.